Couples

A Record Book of Our Love

Artwork by
robbin rawlings

Written by Elena Luz Gómez

Couples

A Record Book of Our Love

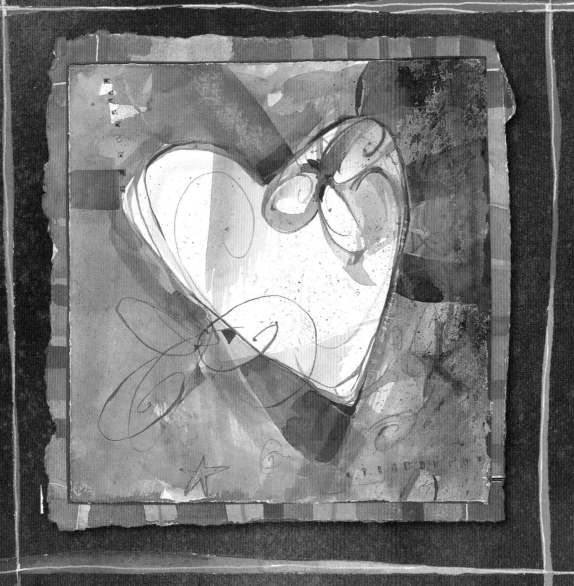

A record book to treasure
for

Vaughn   &   Kristy

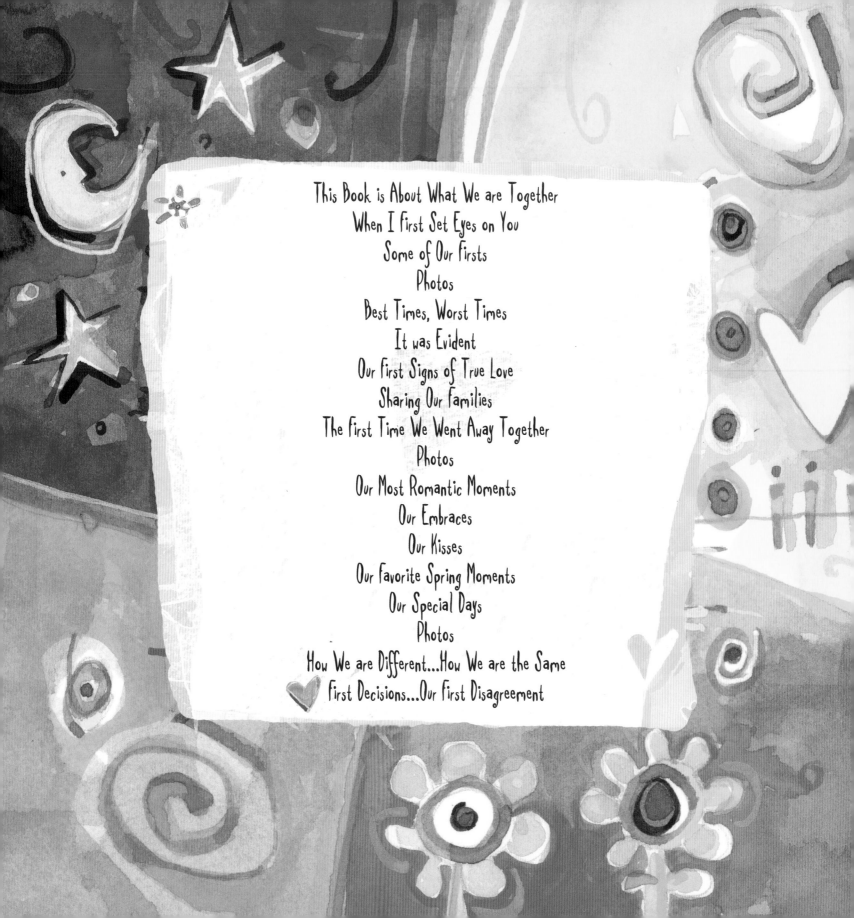

Our Favorite Summer Moments

What it is She Loves About Him

What it is He Loves About Her

Photos

Words are Not Always Easy to Come by...

Those Loving Things We Call Each Other

There are Things We Love to Do Together...

There are Things We Do on Our Own

Our Favorite Fall Moments

The Greatest Triumphs We've Shared

The Great Tragedies We've Shared

Photos

Romance, the Best Appetizer...Love, the Ultimate Main Course

When I'm with You, Music Fills the Air

Our Favorite Winter Moments

When We Go Out

However, When We Stay at Home

And Now, for the Rest of Our Lives

This Book is About
What We are Together

Before him, her life was,...

_____

_____

_____

_____

_____

This is her, without him

She was looking for these traits in a man...

_____

_____

_____

_____

Then suddenly, love happens. You don't have to try.

This is him. Without her

Before her, his life was...

_____

_____

_____

_____

_____

_____

He was looking for these traits in a woman...

_____

_____

_____

_____

_____

When I First Set Eyes on You

He saw a light, sweet and true...

_____

_____

_____

_____

_____

She saw a tenderness, a promise, a sanctuary...

_____

_____

_____

_____

_____

I look into your eyes
and see myself looking
tenderly at you

It was magical, the way we met. It goes like this...

My ex-boyfriend was one of
Vaughn's friends.

What attracted her...

What attracted him...

Some of Our Firsts

I remember our first date, it was
_____

and it was so special because of you, and because...
_____

_____

The first flower he ever gave her...
_____

_____

_____

Our first walk in the rain...
_____

_____ Down the shore in Sea Isle (July 2002) on the _____

boardwalk during the day.

Love: don't be afraid to seize it

Our first long talk...

Was when I was drunk one night and got on the computer & he was online too.

Remembering our first car ride...

The first time we held hands...

I just remember trying to hold his hand & he pulled away, cause "we" were still a secret.

Photo

Photo

Best Times

The best time so far, that which is so special to her and that which she holds close to her heart...

_____

_____

_____

What he says about that time...

_____

_____

_____

Wild things we did. We had so much fun...

_____

_____

_____

Worst Times

Our worst time, one we will look back and laugh at, was special in its own way...

Driving home from the Poconos – he was driving and we got lost... And my 23rd Birthday in A.C.!!!!

How he saw it... Poconos – typical guy doesn't want to ask for directions.

Birthday – He doesn't know how he took care of me – he was a mess too!

Are you as amazed as I am
that I found a love so true
an unexpected surprise
in you

It was evident

She knew she loved him when...

_____

_____

_____

He knew he loved her when...

_____

_____

_____

The best kind of love
is the unexpected

Our First Signs of True Love

Love gives no warning.
Before you know it, swoosh!
You're whisked away.

This is what he did that made her so warm inside...

_____

_____

_____

_____

_____

Her love came through with...

_____

_____

_____

_____

Sharing Our Families

The first time she met his family was on _____

This is how she thought it went... _____

_____

_____

_____

_____

The first time he met her family was on _____

This is how he thought it went... _____

_____

_____

_____

Everything of yours, I love

His loved ones had this to say about her...

_____

_____

_____

_____

_____

Her loved ones had to say this about him...

_____

_____

_____

_____

The First Time We Went Away Together

We threw caution to the wind and on
_____

We went to...
_____
_____

Here We are!

The sun was within me
I had you in my eyes

Some of the best things about that trip were you, me, and...

_____

_____

_____

_____

_____

_____

_____

_____

_____

_____

Photo

Photo

Our most Romantic Moments

Romance develops and changes throughout our life. In the beginning, our idea of romance was...

_____

_____

_____

Our most romantic evening was...

_____

_____

_____

The most romantic telephone conversation was about...

_____

_____

_____

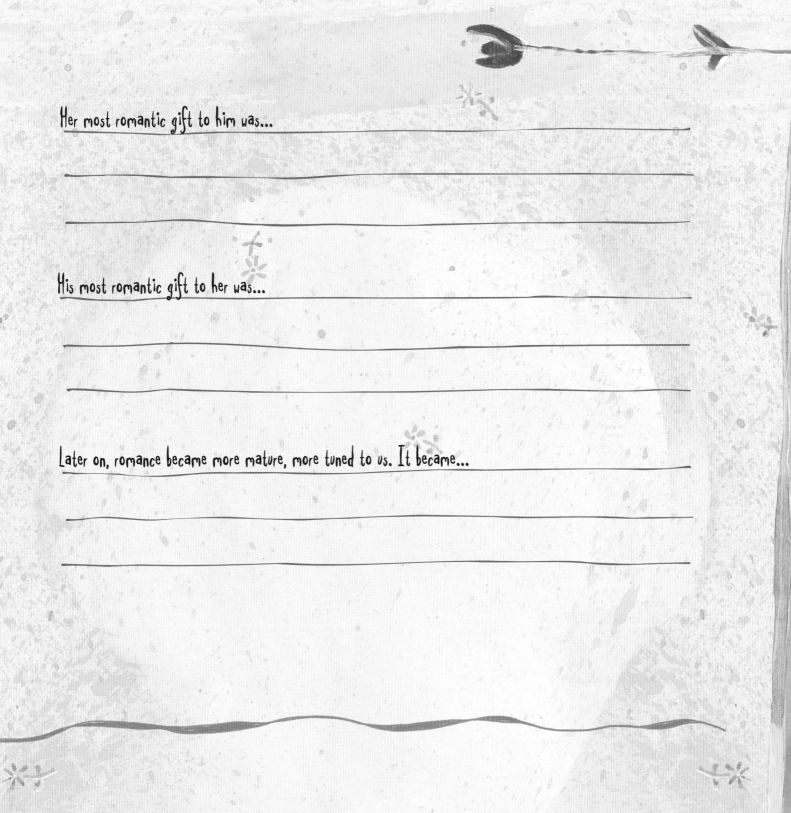

Her most romantic gift to him was...

_____

_____

_____

His most romantic gift to her was...

_____

_____

_____

Later on, romance became more mature, more tuned to us. It became...

_____

_____

_____

There is something about how we hug. Hard to put into words, but it's something like this...

_____

_____

And our kisses, what is it that sets them apart? I think it is...

_____

_____

Our first embrace happened...

_____

_____

_____

_____

Our Kisses

Our first kiss happened...

_____

_____

_____

_____

_____

Our longest kiss was inspired by...

_____

_____

_____

_____

_____

Our Favorite Spring Moments

These are the special things we like to do during the spring months...

_____

_____

_____

_____

_____

_____

Special days we celebrate during spring...

_____

_____

_____

Our favorite springtime memory is...

_____

_____

_____

sring

_____

_____

_____

_____

_____

_____

_____

_____

Photo

Ours is a
springtime love
all year long

Our Special Days

Every day is a celebration, but these are the official ones...

_____

_____

_____

Her birthday is _____

How she likes to celebrate... _____

_____

_____

His birthday is _____

How he likes to celebrate... _____

_____

Our favorite anniversaries...

_____

_____

_____

The most special day of the year for us is...

_____

_____

_____

This is what we do then...

_____

_____

_____

Love at every moment

Photo

Photo

How We are Different

There are some special things that make us different. These are just a few...

_____

_____

_____

These are some of those things she loves...

_____

_____

_____

These are some of those things he loves...

_____

_____

_____

How We are the Same

There are some special things that we have in common. These are just a few...

_____

_____

_____

These are some of those things she loves...

_____

_____

These are some of those things he loves...

_____

_____

_____

First Decisions

All that is good and fair,
pure in light, sweet and true
happens because of love

The first things we purchased together...

_____

_____

_____

That first major decision we made together...

_____

_____

_____

How she felt about it...

_____

_____

_____

How he felt about it...

_____

_____

_____

Our First Disagreement

What it was about...

_____

_____

_____

How we resolved it; how we compromised...

_____

_____

_____

This is how that made us stronger as a couple...

_____

_____

_____

Our love will go on.
and on. and on...

Our Favorite Summer Moments

These are the special things we like to do during the summer months...

_____

_____

_____

_____

_____

_____

_____

Special days we celebrate during summer...

_____

_____

Photo

Our favorite summer memory is...

_____

_____

_____

_____

_____

_____

_____

_____

_____

_____

_____

I love a sleepy
soft sensual day
with you

What it is
She Loves
About Him

She considers these the best parts of his personality...

_____

_____

_____

What she loves about him...

_____

_____

_____

Funny things he says...

_____

_____

_____

What it is He Loves About Her

Photo

He considers these her best traits...

_____

_____

_____

What he loves about her personality...

_____

_____

_____

Funny things she says...

_____

I love so many things about you

_____

Photo

Photo

Words are Not Always Easy to come by

She knows he knows...but she always wanted to tell him that...

_____

_____

_____

_____

_____

He knows she knows, but he always wanted to say...

_____

_____

_____

_____

_____

Love's greatest
nourishments
are time
and attention

Those Loving Things
We Call Each Other

Open my heart,
you'll find
your name
written all over it

She loves his name, but sometimes she calls him...

_____

_____

_____

_____

_____

_____

Her name is music to him, but sometimes he calls her...

_____

_____

_____

_____

_____

There are Things We Love to Do Together

Some of the things she enjoys doing with him...

_____

_____

_____

Some of the things he enjoys doing with her...

_____

_____

_____

There are Things We Do on Our Own

Some of the things she enjoys doing alone...

_____

_____

_____

Some of the things he enjoys doing alone...

_____

_____

_____

Sometimes
Where you are, I know not.
But that you are mine, I'm sure

Our Favorite Fall Moments

These are the special things we like to do during the fall months...

_____

_____

_____

_____

_____

_____

_____

_____

Special days we celebrate during fall...

_____

_____

_____

fall

Your love has been my deepest breath.
Your faith has been cool water for my thirst.

Our favorite fall memory...

Photo

The Great Triumphs We've Shared

The most wonderful things that happened to her...

_____

_____

_____

How he helped her celebrate...

_____

_____

_____

The most wonderful things that happened to him...

_____

_____

_____

How she helped him celebrate...

_____

_____

_____

The Great Tragedies We've Shared

Trials and tribulations we all must live through...

_____
_____
_____
_____
_____
_____
_____

How we helped each other cope...

_____
_____

My hand is there
if you stumble
so if you soar
don't forget
to take it as well

We love hearing from you

havoc®

PUBLISHING

www.havocpub.com

Name: _____

Address: _____

Phone #: _____

E-mail Address: _____

Which is your age group (please circle):

Pre-Teen   Teens   20's   30's   40's   50's   60's   70+

What did you buy/receive ? _____

Where did you buy it ? _____

Comments: _____

Mail To:

HAVOC PUBLISHING
9808 Waples Street
San Diego, California 92121
U.S.A.

Place
Stamp
Here

Photo

Romance, the Best Appetizer

Our favorite foods are...

_____

_____

_____

What he loves to make for her...

_____

_____

_____

What she loves to make for him...

_____

_____

_____

Before him, she never knew about...

_____

_____

_____

Before her, he never knew about...

_____

_____

_____

Foods she doesn't like, but will eat because of him...

_____

_____

_____

Foods he doesn't like, but will eat because of her...

_____

_____

When I'm With You, Music Fills the Air

Music is a big part of our lives. Some of our favorite songs are...

_____

_____

The first song we heard together...

_____

_____

_____

The first time we danced...

_____

_____

What she remembers about it...

_____

_____

What he remembers about it...

_____

_____

His favorite group is...

_____

_____

_____

Her favorite group is...

_____

_____

_____

How our collection of music has grown! Some of our favorite music is...

_____

_____

_____

Some music we grew to like together...

_____

_____

_____

You give me a feeling
of calm, tranquil love

Our Favorite Winter Moments

These are the special things we like to do during the winter months...

_____

_____

_____

_____

_____

Special days we celebrate during winter...

_____

_____

_____

_____

_____

winter

Our favorite winter memory is...

Photo

When We Go out

Our times together are so special. Our favorite things to do when we go out are...

_____

_____

He had never been to...

_____

_____

_____

She had never been to...

_____

_____

_____

Since you came into my life
a brightness like
new morning embraces me

Our favorite restaurant..._____

Our favorite movie theater..._____

Our favorite spot to hang out..._____

However, When We Stay at Home

Our favorite things to do at home are...

_____

_____

_____

We gaze into each other's eyes
to pierce the thin veil
between the eye and the soul

What we munch on...

_____

_____

_____

First movie we saw together...

_____

_____

_____

Games we like to play...

_____

_____

_____

And Now, for the Rest of Our Lives

What she really wants for the future...

_____

_____

_____

_____

_____

_____

_____

_____

Does anyone who loves
this way forget?

All I pray for is
always a tomorrow
with you

What he really wants for the future...